The Legacy of Letting Go

A Journal for Those Healing from Love That Could Not Stay

By: **Katerina Markadakis**

Epigraph

*"Healing begins when we stop running from what still hurts
and learn to sit beside it instead."*

— K.M.

Publisher: Harbor Point Press — Seaford, New York

The Legacy Series Note

A collection of soul-centered journals exploring the evolution of love, loss, and self-return. Each volume marks a stage in remembrance, from the ache of release to the peace of becoming.

Titles in the Series:

1. *The Legacy of Letting Go* — *Releasing what was heavy*
2. *The Legacy of Silence* — *Learning to listen within*
3. *The Legacy of Longing* — *Reclaiming desire and depth*
4. *The Legacy of Healing* — *Meeting forgiveness with grace*
5. *The Legacy of Becoming* — *Returning home to yourself*

Together, they tell one story:
how love, once lost, became light.

Legacy Continuum Introduction

How *The Legacy of Letting Go* Began It All

Every Legacy was born from this one, the moment I realized love and loss could coexist. The Legacy of Letting Go began as a whisper, a way to name what could not stay.

What started as heartbreak became a healing language, **one that others could speak as well.**

From these pages, the Continuum unfolded — Silence, Longing, Healing, Becoming — each one a new way of returning to myself.

This book holds the origin wound — **the breaking open that birthed all others.**

It is not the end of love, it is the beginning of awareness.

Expanded Legacy Series Note

From Page to Healing

These journals were never meant to be stories;
they were meant to be mirrors.

Each page began as a letter I wrote to the parts of myself I
once abandoned in love.

I wrote until the ache softened,
until I could look at the silence and see understanding instead
of shame.

I wrote until healing no longer felt like a destination,
but a devotion.

If you are holding this, it is because your heart recognized
itself.

Let this be your permission to begin again,
not by chasing closure, but by choosing presence.

Preface

When I started writing about avoidance, I was trying to understand why some people run from love.

What I learned is that most of us aren't running from others — we're running from the feeling of being unworthy of staying.

If you've ever felt safer in distance than in closeness, this journal is for you.

It's a space to meet the part of you that still hides when things feel too real.

Move slowly.

There's no rush here.

Each reflection is an open door — step through only when you're ready.

Healing has its own rhythm, and it will always wait for you.

Dedication

For the ones who loved through silence.
For the hearts that stayed soft in the face of withdrawal.
For those who waited, and then learned to wait no more.

May you find yourself in these pages —
not as the one who was left,
but as the one who finally came home.

Author's Note

Dear Reader,

You began this journal not to fix yourself,
but to understand yourself,
to meet the parts of you that once hid behind independence
and composure.

Avoidance is not a flaw;
it is a language your heart learned to survive.
But now,
you are learning a new language, one of presence,
vulnerability, and repair.

You have done something sacred:
you turned toward what once terrified you.
You stayed.
And in doing so,
you have rewritten the legacy.

May these pages remind you, always,
that awareness is not punishment, it is freedom;
that connection is not danger, it is healing;
that love is not a performance, it is practice.

And that you, too,
are capable of staying.

With gentleness and reverence,
Katerina Markadakis

★ ★ ★

Understanding the Avoidant Heart

There are some who love in a distance — not because they
do not care,
but because closeness once felt like danger.

The avoidant heart was not born cold; **it was built for self-
protection.**
Where love should have felt safe, it felt consuming.
Where connection should have brought warmth, it brought
overwhelm.

So they learned to retreat —
to stay near enough to feel affection,
but far enough to breathe.

This knowing is not an excuse;
it is a compassion that keeps your heart from hardening.

You are allowed to grieve what they could not give,
and still understand that their fear of intimacy was never your
fault.

You could not have stayed soft enough to make them stay.
But you can stay soft enough to keep your own heart open.

Welcome to Your Journey of Healing and Self-Discovery

This is not a book about forgetting.
It is a journey of remembering — of tracing the thread of
your love back to yourself.

You will not find instructions here.
You will find reflection, breath, and truth.

Let every word meet you softly.
Let the pages hold what your hands can't yet release.

You may return to this book many times — as you grieve, as
you awaken, as you grow.
It will read differently each time,
because you will be different each time.

Healing is not linear.
It is cyclical — a spiral that brings you home by way of
everything you thought you lost.

Preface – The Pattern That Broke You

There is a kind of love that teaches you everything you never
wanted to know about absence.
It is the love that starts in warmth and ends in silence —
the kind that makes you question if you imagined it all.

You replay moments like prayers,
wondering how something that felt so safe could turn into
distance so quickly.

This book is for those who loved an avoidant heart —
those who stayed soft when someone else went still,
who kept showing up for conversations that never came.

You did not break because you loved deeply.
You broke because you kept loving in one direction.

This is not about blame;
it is about release.
It is a reclamation of your self-worth,
a slow unbinding of all the ways you learned to chase, prove,
wait, and ache.

You are not here to understand them anymore.
You are here to remember you.

Because what you gave was sacred —
and it deserves to come home.

Table Of Contents

PART I THE INHERITANCE OF SILENCE 1

    When Love Teaches You to Stay Quiet...............................1

    Reflection Prompts 2

    The Body Remembers What Love Taught It.......................4

    Affirmation...5

PART II – THE WEIGHT OF WAITING........................6

    When Hope Becomes a Habit..6

    The Wounds of Absence..7

    The Cycle of Almost...8

    Reflection Prompts 9

    The Truth About Patience 11

    When You Finally Let Go.. 12

    Affirmation.. 13

PART III – THE TURNING INWARD 14

    Coming Home to Yourself After Being Left Emotionally
Unmet 14

    Reclaiming the Self That Waited..................................... 15

    The Nervous System of Safety 16

    Reflection Prompts 17

    The Practice of Reconnection 19

    The Mirror of Inner Love... 20

    Affirmation.. 21

    The Nervous System and Love.. 22

PART IV – BOUNDARIES AS HEALING 23

Rebuilding Safety Without Shutting Down 23

The Myth of "Too Much 24

Reflection Prompts 25

Boundaries Are Love, Too 27

Relearning Connection 28

A Gentle Reminder 29

Affirmation 30

Release Ritual – Letting Go with Ceremony 31

PART V – THE REBIRTH OF SELF-WORTH 32

Remembering the You Who Existed Before the Waiting 32

The Soft Return 33

The Myth of Earning Love 34

Reflection Prompts 35

Becoming the Safe Place 37

A Note on Forgiveness 38

Affirmation 39

PART VI – THE LEGACY YOU CHOOSE 40

Turning Pain Into Wisdom and Presence Into Peace 40

The Ending That Becomes a Beginning 41

The Legacy of Presence 42

Reflection Prompts 43

Letting the Past Rest 45

Your New Legacy 46

The Unlearning & Rebuilding Inner Safety.......................... 47

Affirmation.. 48

Afterword – For the One Who Finally Chose Herself..... 49

Closing Blessing... 51

Practices for Presence (Healing Appendix – to be placed near the end of the book)... 52

Blessing For The Journey Ahead...................................... 54

About the Author.. 55

PART I
THE INHERITANCE OF SILENCE

When Love Teaches You to Stay Quiet

Before you learned how to love with hope,
you learned how to love with silence.
Perhaps from a parent who was kind but unreachable,
or from a world that taught you to earn your place
through patience, perfection, or peacekeeping.

You didn't become drawn to avoidance by accident —
you were trained to find comfort in emotional distance.
It felt familiar, even when it hurt.

Avoidant love mirrors the earliest lesson:
that love may come but not stay,
that your needs may be too heavy to hold.

So, you made yourself lighter.
You learned to smile instead of speak,
to understand instead of ask,
to make your pain small enough
that no one else would have to carry it.

And yet, that very silence became the soil of your loneliness.
You learned to bloom quietly
in places that never saw your full color.

* * *

1. When did you first learn that expressing emotion could lead to withdrawal or rejection?

_____

_____

_____

_____

_____

2. How do you tend to minimize or silence your needs in relationships?

_____

_____

_____

_____

_____

3. What forms of attention or affection do you settle for because full presence feels unavailable?

_____

_____

_____

_____

_____

4. How would it feel to be fully seen and not have to earn it?

_____

_____

_____

_____

_____

* * *

The Body Remembers What Love Taught It

Your nervous system holds the story of this pattern.
When you loved someone avoidant,
your body learned to wait,
to brace,
to breathe quietly until the next moment of closeness
returned.

You learned to live on crumbs —
not because you lacked worth,
but because you were starving for connection.

Healing means feeding yourself again.
It means reminding your body that love
is not supposed to feel like waiting.

You are not meant to be sustained by fragments;
you are meant to feel full.

★ ★ ★

Affirmation

I no longer chase what withdraws.
I am not a reflection of another's avoidance.
My love was not too much — it was simply unreceived.
I release the silence that kept me small.
I am ready to speak, to feel, to heal.

★ ★ ★

PART II – THE WEIGHT OF WAITING

When Hope Becomes a Habit

You learned to wait beautifully —
to fill the empty spaces with meaning,
to soften your voice so they wouldn't pull away,
to convince yourself that patience was love.

But love should not feel like holding your breath.

Waiting became your rhythm —
waiting for a reply, a change, a sign, a moment of tenderness.
You built altars of hope in every silence,
believing that if you just held on a little longer,
they would come back different this time.

You mistook endurance for devotion.
You thought that staying proved your love's strength.
But in truth, it only proved your tolerance for being unseen.

And that is not the same as being loved.

* * *

The Wounds of Absence

There are wounds that never bled —
the kind that live in pauses and half-kept promises.

Avoidance leaves no scars, only echoes.
You begin to mistake distance for peace,
until silence feels safer than truth.

These are the wounds of absence —
the quiet spaces where love was meant to live.

You learned to nurture emptiness, to hold on to almosts,
to translate inconsistency into care.

But absence is not love's language;
it is love unspoken.

You are allowed to stop listening for what will not return.

★ ★ ★

The Cycle of Almost

Avoidant love teaches you to live in the almost.
Almost close.
Almost known.
Almost chosen.

You feel a connection in glimpses —
tiny moments when their guard drops and the warmth
returns.
Your nervous system lights up:
"See? They do care. Maybe we're okay."

But then it fades again.
The texts grow sparse, the tone distant,
and your body braces for the drop —
the quiet rejection that feels like your fault.

You begin to believe love is something you must manage:
if you stay calm enough,
if you say the right thing,
if you don't need too much,
they will stay.

This is the exhaustion no one sees —
the emotional labor of loving someone who lives half inside
their own walls.

But you cannot heal by waiting for someone who fears
closeness.
You heal by walking out of the waiting room.

★ ★ ★

1.   What are you still waiting for — a message, an apology, a version of them that never arrives?

_____

_____

_____

_____

_____

2.   What do you tell yourself when someone pulls away?

_____

_____

_____

_____

_____

3.   How does waiting make you feel safe — and how does it keep you stuck?

_____

_____

_____

_____

_____

4. What would you gain if you stopped waiting and started choosing yourself?

_____

_____

_____

_____

_____

★ ★ ★

The Truth About Patience

You are not unworthy because they could not meet you.
You are not "too much."
You are simply ready — and they are not.

You cannot teach someone to stay who has not yet learned
how to be with themselves.
You cannot heal someone by abandoning yourself in the
process.

Patience is a virtue when it is shared.
But when it is one-sided,
it becomes a wound.

You do not need to be calm in someone else's chaos
if it costs you your peace.

Sometimes closure is not a conversation;
it's the quiet decision to stop waiting.

★ ★ ★

When you stop waiting,
something strange happens:
the silence stops feeling personal.

You begin to see that their withdrawal was never about your
worth;
it was their fear speaking through absence.

And in that awareness,
you start to reclaim every piece of yourself you left in their
pauses.

Letting go is not the end of love —
it is the end of confusion.
It is the beginning of clarity.

★ ★ ★

Affirmation

I release the need to be chosen by those who fear closeness.
I no longer confuse silence with peace.
My patience is sacred — it deserves reciprocity.
I will no longer wait where my heart is not met.
I am ready to move from hoping to healing.

★ ★ ★

PART III – THE TURNING INWARD

Coming Home to Yourself After Being Left Emotionally Unmet

Healing begins in the same place avoidance ends —
inside silence.
But this time, it's a silence that nourishes, not empties.

For so long, you gave your love outward.
You poured tenderness into someone who could not receive
it.
You learned to survive on echoes and almosts.

Now, that energy comes home.

Turning inward is not giving up;
it is remembering that your heart was never meant to orbit
another person's fear.
It was meant to root in your own soil,
to bloom where your care is returned.

★ ★ ★

Reclaiming the Self That Waited

There is a version of you still sitting in that waiting room —
the one who hoped, explained, softened, and stayed.

Go to her.
Place your hand over your heart and whisper,
"You did your best with what you knew."

You were never foolish for loving.
You were brave for believing in connection.
But now, your bravery looks different.
It is no longer endurance — it is release.

You do not have to prove your worth through patience
anymore.
You are allowed to take your love back from the ones who
could not hold it.

* * *

When you love someone avoidant, your body learns to brace.
The on-and-off pattern trains your nervous system to live
between hope and panic.
Your heart beats in uncertainty; your mind spins in "What did
I do wrong?"

Now that you are turning inward, your work is to remind
your body
that the threat is gone.

Healing is not just mental clarity — it is physical safety.
It's letting your shoulders drop for the first time in months.
It's breathing without waiting for the phone to light up.

This is what safety feels like:

- predictable rhythms
- self-chosen quiet
- the absence of confusion
- the return of calm

Your peace no longer depends on someone else's
consistency; it lives in your own steadiness.

★ ★ ★

Reflection Prompts

1. What parts of yourself did you abandon while waiting for love to return?

_____

_____

_____

_____

_____

2. What does emotional safety mean to you — and when did you last feel it?

_____

_____

_____

_____

_____

3. How can you begin to give yourself the reassurance you used to seek from them?

_____

_____

_____

_____

_____

4. What new rituals or moments of stillness make your body feel like home again?

_____

_____

_____

_____

_____

* * *

The Practice of Reconnection

Try this:
When you feel the pull of longing — that ache that says
maybe they'll come back —
place your hand on your heart and breathe slowly.

Inhale for four counts, exhale for six.
Say softly:
"I am here. I am safe. I am no longer waiting."

Repeat it until your breath steadies.
This is what it feels like to re-parent yourself —
to offer the safety no one else could.

Every time you choose stillness over chasing,
you are building a new nervous system —
one that no longer confuses anxiety for connection.

★ ★ ★

The Mirror of Inner Love

You spent so long looking outward for validation,
but your healing begins the moment you turn the mirror
around.

Ask yourself:

- What makes me feel loved when I'm alone?
- What part of me needs attention right now?
- What would I say to the version of me who begged to be
seen?

And then, say it.
Say everything you needed to hear.

You are the one who stays now.

★ ★ ★

Affirmation

I am no longer waiting for peace to find me.
I am learning to build it inside myself.

I am safe in my own presence.
I am gentle with my own heart.

I no longer chase what left —
I return to what remains:
me.

★ ★ ★

The Nervous System and Love

The body remembers the rhythm of uncertainty.
Every unanswered message, every sudden silence —
your pulse recorded them like small alarms.

Avoidant love activates the oldest reflex:
"If I am calm, maybe they will return."
But healing means retraining that instinct.

Each time you breathe through the wave instead of reaching
outward,
you teach your nervous system a new story:

"I can feel fear and still be safe."

Your body is not broken;
it is learning to stop mistaking tension for tenderness.
Be patient with the physical ache that comes as you unlearn
survival.
Peace is a muscle too — and it strengthens with practice.

★ ★ ★

PART IV – BOUNDARIES AS HEALING

$$\bullet\!\!-\!\!-\!\!-\!\!\diamond\!\!\blacklozenge\!\!\diamond\!\!-\!\!-\!\!-\!\!\bullet$$

Rebuilding Safety Without Shutting Down

You once believed that love meant access —
that being open meant never saying no,
that to keep someone close, you had to stay available,
forgiving, and patient.

But now you know:
love without boundaries is self-abandonment disguised as
care.

Boundaries are not rejection;
they are clarity.
They say, "This is where I end and where you begin."
They allow love to breathe without suffocating either heart.

When you loved an avoidant,
you learned to shrink so the distance between you wouldn't
feel so big.
You made yourself smaller, quieter, easier to love.
You thought if you didn't take up too much space,
they would have room to stay.

But you deserve to take up space in your own story.

★ ★ ★

The Myth of "Too Much"

Every time you felt ignored or dismissed,
you translated that pain into self-blame.
"Maybe I'm too emotional. Too sensitive. Too needy."

You were never too much.
You were simply asking for consistency in a place that could
not offer it.

Avoidant love thrives in your silence —
it needs your self-denial to survive.
But your healing thrives in truth.
Your voice, your needs, your limits — they are not burdens;
they are bridges.

You are not asking for too much;
you are asking the wrong person to give it.

★ ★ ★

1. What boundaries did you break within yourself to keep someone else close?

_____

_____

_____

_____

_____

2. When you think of saying "no," what feelings rise — guilt, fear, or relief?

_____

_____

_____

_____

_____

3. How might your relationships shift if your needs were treated as sacred, not shameful?

_____

_____

_____

_____

_____

4. What would it feel like to protect your peace as fiercely as you protected their comfort?

_____

_____

_____

_____

_____

★ ★ ★

Boundaries Are Love, Too

You were taught that saying no pushes people away,
but healthy love understands no as honesty, not rejection.

When you honor your boundaries,
you invite relationships built on respect, not fear.

A partner who values closeness will never ask you to trade
your truth for their comfort.
And a partner who disappears when you set boundaries
was never planning to stay for love — only for control.

So let them go.
Let silence replace negotiation.
Let your boundary be your closure.

You don't need to prove your worth by breaking yourself
open for those who cannot meet you.

★ ★ ★

Relearning Connection

Healing does not mean closing off;
it means choosing where your energy flows.
You can be open and discerning, soft and strong.

The more you respect your boundaries,
the more your nervous system learns that love does not have
to mean danger.

Boundaries are how you teach your body what safety feels
like.
Every time you honor your limits,
you send your heart the message:

"I am safe now. I can trust myself."

And that trust — that inner safety —
is what makes true intimacy possible again.

★ ★ ★

A Gentle Reminder

You do not have to be understood by those who need you
silent to feel secure.
You do not have to explain boundaries to people committed
to crossing them.

Healing is not convincing others to change;
it is choosing yourself, even when it confuses them.

You are not walking away from love —
you are walking toward peace.

★ ★ ★

Affirmation

My boundaries are bridges, not walls.
They guide love toward safety, not away from it.

I no longer abandon myself to keep others comfortable.
I honor my truth, even when it trembles.

My no is sacred.
My peace is protection.
My worth is nonnegotiable.

★ ★ ★

There are endings that don't arrive with words — only with quiet knowing.

You've analyzed, explained, forgiven, and cried.

Now, you are ready to release.

This ritual is not for closure from another;

it's for your spirit — a sacred way to mark that you are no longer waiting.

The Release Ritual:

1. Light a candle or sit by a window where the light can touch you.
2. Write a letter to the person, or the version of yourself, you've been trying to save.
3. Read it out loud. Say everything — the pain, the hope, the truth.
4. When you finish, whisper:
   "I set you free, and I set myself free too."
5. Fold the letter and place it somewhere safe, or burn it carefully.
   Watch the smoke rise. Feel the space it leaves behind.

You are not burning love — you are burning the weight that kept you from it.

This is how you let go — not in anger, but in peace.

★ ★ ★

PART V – THE REBIRTH OF SELF-WORTH

Remembering the You Who Existed Before the Waiting

There comes a moment in every healing when the ache
begins to quiet —
not because you have forgotten,
but because you have finally remembered yourself.

For so long, your reflection was shaped by someone else's
distance.
Their silence became the mirror you measured your value
against.
Now, you are breaking that mirror.

You are seeing yourself with new eyes —
not as someone who wasn't enough,
but as someone who gave too much love to someone who
could not hold it.

You are not broken;
you are unlearning depletion.

★ ★ ★

The Soft Return

Rebirth is not loud.
It doesn't arrive in grand gestures or sudden confidence.
It begins in quiet decisions —
to wake without checking your phone,
to smile at your own reflection,
to eat when you're hungry, rest when you're tired,
to stop apologizing for existing with emotion.

Healing does not rush;
it unfolds the way flowers open —
in their own time, in their own season,
toward the light they finally trust.

Every act of self-care is a declaration:

"I am worth tending to."

You are not rebuilding yourself;
you are remembering who you have always been.

★ ★ ★

The Myth of Earning Love

You were taught that love must be earned —
through goodness, patience, performance, or perfection.

But true love cannot be bargained for;
it must be received.

You do not need to become smaller to be held.
You do not need to dim your joy to be kept.
You do not need to chase anyone who cannot see you.

Your worth was never dependent on their awareness of it.
It is the constant that remains
after everything temporary has fallen away.

★ ★ ★

Reflection Prompts

1. What are the quiet ways you've already begun to return to
yourself?

_____

_____

_____

_____

_____

2. How have you confused being chosen with being worthy?

_____

_____

_____

_____

_____

3. What parts of yourself do you now want to celebrate
rather than hide?

_____

_____

_____

_____

_____

4. How can you begin to nurture joy without waiting for permission or reciprocation?

_____

_____

_____

_____

* * *

Becoming the Safe Place

You spent years trying to find safety in someone else's
steadiness.
Now, you are becoming the safe place you sought.

Self-worth is not an idea — it is a practice.
It is how you speak to yourself when you are lonely.
It is how you hold your own disappointment without
punishment.
It is how you honor your emotions without apologizing for
them.

You no longer need someone else to validate your softness;
you are learning to witness it yourself.

This is the moment where the energy shifts —
from longing to embodiment,
from surviving to living.

You are no longer defined by who left;
you are defined by how you stayed —
with yourself.

★ ★ ★

A Note on Forgiveness

Forgiveness does not mean returning;
it means freeing your body from the weight of resentment.
You forgive not because they deserve peace,
but because you do.

Letting go is not weakness;
it is a sacred act of closure.

Every time you release the story of what could have been,
you make space for what still can be.

★ ★ ★

Affirmation

I am whole, even with the scars.
I am worthy, even without their validation.

My joy is not dependent on being chosen.
My peace does not require permission.

I am no longer defined by who left;
I am defined by who I have become.

I am the love I was always waiting for.

★ ★ ★

PART VI – THE LEGACY YOU CHOOSE

Turning Pain Into Wisdom and Presence Into Peace

You came here to heal a pattern — not just in your lifetime, but in the lineage of all the women who waited before you.

The ones who loved through silence,
who spoke gently so as not to be left,
who carried others' emotions while abandoning their own.

You are the one who said, "It ends here."

You are the bridge between old pain and new peace.
You are not repeating the story — you are rewriting it.

★ ★ ★

The Ending That Becomes a Beginning

There will come a day when you look back and realize
that the love which broke you
was also the love that began to free you.

Because it woke something ancient inside you —
the part that remembered its worth.

Avoidant love forced you to learn boundaries.
Inconsistency taught you to find safety in yourself.
Loss taught you to become whole without proof.

You did not lose because they left.
You found because you stayed.

You stayed for your healing.
You stayed for your peace.
You stayed for the woman you were always becoming.

This is your legacy:
the courage to remain present in a world that told you to
disappear.

★ ★ ★

The Legacy of Presence

You are no longer passing down silence;
you are passing down truth.
You are no longer teaching others that love requires
shrinking;
you are teaching that love is allowed to expand.

When you honor your boundaries,
when you speak your needs,
when you choose a connection that feels calm instead of
chaotic,
you are creating a new inheritance —
one where love no longer means loss.

You are becoming the kind of person
who makes safety feel like home.

★ ★ ★

1. What patterns of love and self-abandonment end with you?

_____

_____

_____

_____

_____

2. What values do you want your future relationships — or your children, your friends, your heart — to inherit from you?

_____

_____

_____

_____

_____

3. What does lasting, grounded love look like to you now — not a fantasy, but a felt reality?

_____

_____

_____

_____

_____

4. How will you honor the peace you fought to build?

_____

_____

_____

_____

_____

Letting the Past Rest

You do not need to keep returning to what hurt you
to prove that you have healed.

The wound is no longer the story — **the healing is.**
The silence is no longer your home — **the peace is.**

You can release the longing,
not by pretending it never mattered,
but by thanking it for what it taught you.

Because everything you went through brought you here —
to the steadiness of your own presence.

That is the most radical form of closure.

★ ★ ★

Your New Legacy

You are no longer a reflection of someone else's fear of
closeness.
You are a mirror of love that stays.

You are the keeper of boundaries,
the protector of peace,
the author of your new story.

This is how the legacy shifts:
from distance to devotion,
from silence to expression,
from absence to arrival.

And that arrival —
the way you now stand inside your own heart without
apology —
is everything you came here to learn.

★ ★ ★

The Unlearning & Rebuilding Inner Safety

Healing is not about becoming new — it is about
remembering who you were before fear taught you smallness.

You are unlearning urgency.
You are unlearning apology.
You are unlearning the habit of translating absence into proof
of unworthiness.

To rebuild safety is to teach your body that love does not
have to mean waiting.

Breathe here.
Feel your heartbeat as evidence of belonging.
You are not healing to be chosen again —
you are healing so that you no longer leave yourself.

★ ★ ★

Affirmation

I am not the absence I was given.
I am the presence I have chosen.

I no longer carry the legacy of avoidance.
I carry the legacy of awareness, compassion, and peace.

My love is steady.
My voice is clear.
My boundaries are sacred.

I am the one who stayed.
I am the one who healed.
I am the one who begins again.

★ ★ ★

Dear You,

You did not come here to learn how to be loved better.
You came here to learn how to love yourself differently.

The kind of love you gave was sacred —
pure, hopeful, patient —
but it was always meant to lead you home.

You may never get the apology, the closure, or the version of
them who could stay.
But you are getting something infinitely more powerful —
peace.

The Legacy of Letting Go is not just a title; it's a
transformation.
It is the end of confusion and the beginning of clarity.
It is no longer about who didn't see you —
it's about how you finally learned to see yourself.

There will still be moments you miss them.
There will still be days you ache for the softness of what
could have been.
But now, you know how to stay through the ache.
You know how to breathe through the silence.
You know that the love you were waiting for —
was always the love you are capable of giving to yourself.

So when you feel the old pull — to chase, to explain, to wait
—

pause, place your hand over your heart,
and whisper:

"I am here now. I choose me."

With gentleness and grace,
Katerina Markadakis

* * *

Closing Blessing

May you remember that leaving was once survival,
but staying is now strength.

May your love no longer be measured by how much you
endure,
but by how much peace it brings you.

May your boundaries be soft and sure,
your words honest and kind,
your heart brave enough to receive the love that finally feels
safe.

You are the ending of one legacy,
and the beginning of another.

★ ★ ★

Practices for Presence
(Healing Appendix – to be placed near the end of the book)

When you are triggered, lonely, or missing what never fully was, return here.

These small practices are how you build safety — one moment, one breath, one heartbeat at a time.

1. **The Breath**
   Inhale slowly for four counts.
   Exhale for six.
   Place your hand on your chest and whisper:
   "I am safe to stay."
   Repeat until your body believes you.

2. **The Ground**
   Press your feet gently into the floor.
   Feel the earth's quiet support beneath you.
   You are held — even when no one is here to hold you.

3. **The Reframe**
   When the thought comes — "Maybe they'll change" —
   answer softly: **"Maybe I will."**
   You are no longer waiting for someone to return;
   you are returning to yourself.

4. **The Reflection**
   Ask yourself before sleep:
   "What did I do today that honored my healing?"
   It can be small. It all counts.

5. **The Reassurance**
   You are not behind.
   Healing is not linear.
   Every moment you choose peace over panic, you are
   rewriting your nervous system's story.

These are not tasks — they are remembrances.
You are not learning how to love again.
You are remembering that you already know how.

★ ★ ★

Blessing For The Journey Ahead

May the fear that once kept you distant
become the wisdom that keeps you kind.

May your hands learn softness,
your voice learn truth,
your heart learn safety in the company of love.

May you no longer confuse peace with silence
or protection with isolation.

May you feel worthy of being seen,
not for your calm,
not for your control,
but for your humanness.

And when old patterns whisper,
"Leave before you are left,"
may you whisper back,
"I am not leaving. I am learning to stay."

You have broken the inheritance of absence.
You have become the legacy of presence.

★ ★ ★

End of *The Legacy of Letting Go — A Journal for Those Healing from Love That Could Not Stay*

by **Katerina Markadakis**

Katerina Markadakis is the author of The Legacy of Avoidance: For Those Learning to Stay When Love Feels Unsafe and its companion, The Legacy of Avoidance — A Journal for Those Learning to Stay When Love Feels Unsafe.

Through her imprint, Harbor Point Press, she writes both fiction and non-fiction that explore love, loss, and the quiet strength of returning to oneself.

Her Legacy Series — Legacy of Silence, Legacy of Longing, Legacy of Healing, and Legacy of Becoming — reveals how our stories become the mirrors that guide us home.

She is also the author of The Legacy of Letting Go: For Those Healing from Love That Could Not Stay and its companion journal.

Katerina lives in Seaford, New York, where she continues to write and publish under Harbor Point Press, creating books that invite readers to find peace in presence and meaning in the spaces between.

Publisher Imprint Page

Published by Harbor Point Press
Seaford, New York | Est. 2025

ISBN: [To be assigned]